Brands We Know

General Mills

By Sara Green

Bellwether Media • Minneapolis, MN

Jump into the cockpit and take flight with **Pilot** books. Your journey will take you on high-energy adventures as you learn about all that is wild, weird, fascinating, and fun!

This edition first published in 2018 by Bellwether Media, Inc.

No part of this publication may be reproduced in whole or in part without written permission of the publisher.
For information regarding permission, write to Bellwether Media, Inc., Attention: Permissions Department, 5357 Penn Avenue South, Minneapolis, MN 55419.

Library of Congress Cataloging-in-Publication Data

Names: Green, Sara, 1964- author.
Title: General Mills / by Sara Green.
Description: Minneapolis, MN : Bellwether Media, Inc., [2018] | Series: Pilot: Brands We Know | Includes bibliographical references and index. | Audience: Grades 3-8
Identifiers: LCCN 2017012073 (print) | LCCN 2016052727 (ebook) | ISBN 9781626176522 (hardcover : alk. paper) | ISBN 9781681033822 (ebook)
Subjects: LCSH: General Mills, Inc.--Juvenile literature. | Food industry and trade--United States--Juvenile literature.
Classification: LCC HD9009.G47 G74 2018 (ebook) | LCC HD9009.G47 (print) | DDC 338.7/66400973--dc23
LC record available at https://lccn.loc.gov/2017012073

Editor: Betsy Rathburn   Designer: Josh Brink

Printed in the United States of America, North Mankato, MN.

Table of Contents

What Is General Mills? 4

The Rise of Flour Mills 6

Growth and Change 10

Foods People Love Today 14

Serving Others 18

General Mills Timeline 20

Glossary 22

To Learn More 23

Index 24

What Is General Mills?

A family shops for groceries together. Everyone picks a favorite food. One family member tosses a box of Lucky Charms into the cart. Another adds a Totino's Party Pizza. Yoplait yogurt and Nature Valley granola bars go in next. The family remembers to get Betty Crocker cake mix and Häagen-Dazs ice cream to celebrate a coming birthday. These **brands** all come from General Mills!

General Mills, Inc. is an American food company. Its **headquarters** is in Golden Valley, Minnesota. The company makes and sells many well-known brands, including Progresso, Pillsbury, and Fruit Roll-Ups. It is also famous for its breakfast cereals. Cheerios and Cocoa Puffs are favorites. General Mills sells its products on six continents. Its cursive capital G **logo** is recognized around the world. Today, the company is worth more than $30 billion. It is one of the largest food companies on the planet!

Lucky Charms

Nature Valley granola bars

Häagen-Dazs

By the Numbers

over
$16 billion
in sales in 2016

more than
100
countries sell General
Mills products

more than
39,000
employees

more than
$754 million
spent on
advertising in 2016

about
$1 billion
in Cheerios sales
in 2014

more than
$2.6 billion
in breakfast cereal
sales in the United
States in 2016

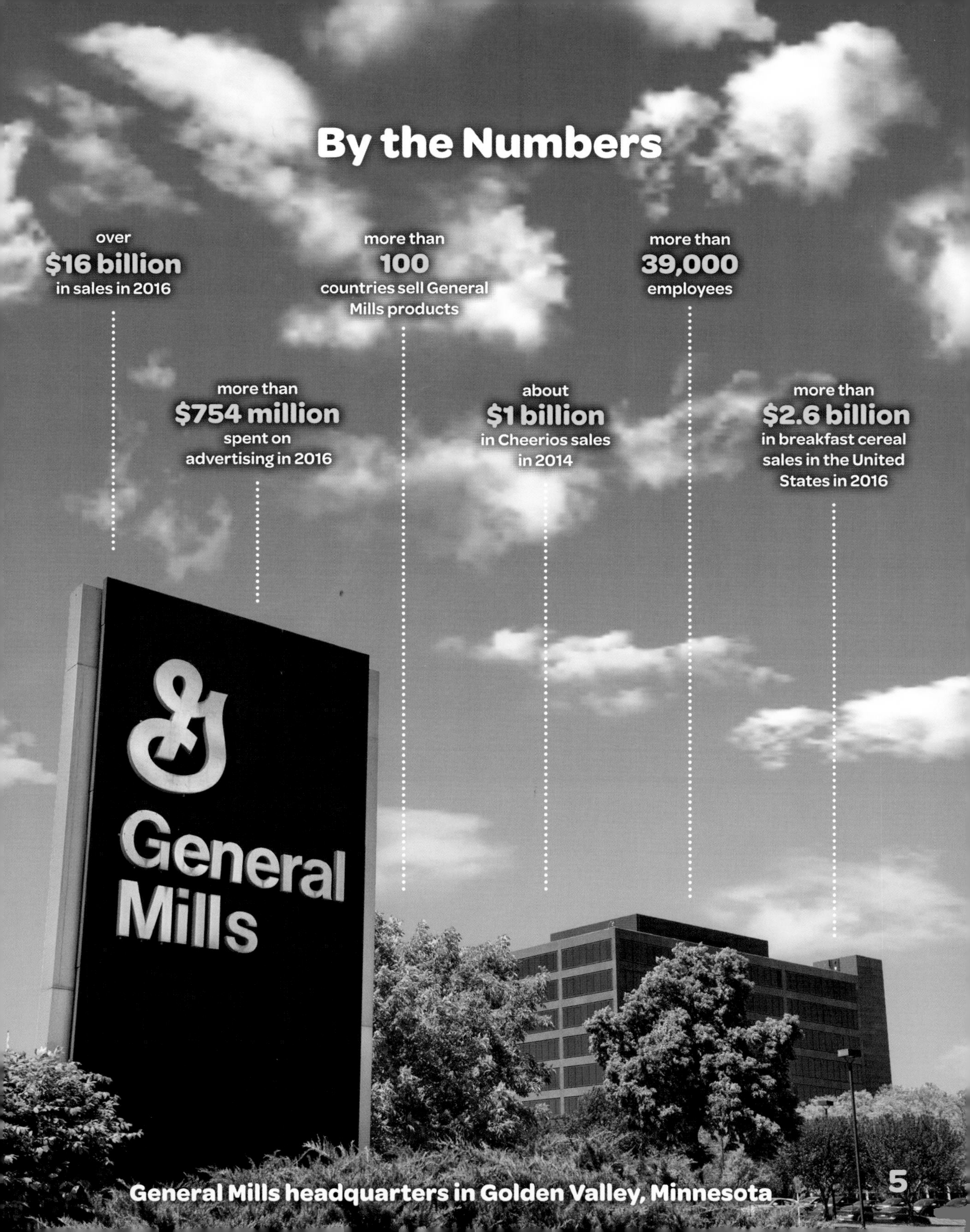

General Mills headquarters in Golden Valley, Minnesota

The Rise of Flour Mills

In 1866, Cadwallader Washburn built a flour mill in Minneapolis, Minnesota. It was located near a waterfall on the Mississippi River. The force of the waterfall powered the mill to grind wheat into flour. Other mills also operated along the river. In time, the millers decided to work as a team to make better flour. This way, they could set prices and control the **market**. In 1876, they formed an organization called the Minneapolis Millers Association. Soon, Minneapolis was known as the flour-milling capital of the world!

A Stately Leader
Cadwallader Washburn was the governor of Wisconsin from 1872 to 1874.

Cadwallader Washburn

Eventually—Why Not Now?

1900s-1940s Gold Medal Flour tagline

Minneapolis, Minnesota

A miller named John Crosby partnered with Cadwallader in 1877. Together, they formed the Washburn Crosby Company. A year later, disaster struck. Their mill caught fire and exploded. The men soon built a new mill that used safer technology. Their flour was better than ever. It won gold, silver, and bronze medals! The top flour was renamed Gold Medal Flour. It is still famous today.

Gold Medal Flour

The late 1800s saw a drop in wheat sales. Some mills were in trouble. But Washburn Crosby continued to grow. By this time, the company's flour was being shipped overseas. More changes were to come. The company created a character named Betty Crocker in 1921. She answered letters and **advertised** for the company. Many people listened to her radio cooking show. It was one of the longest-running radio shows in history!

A man named James Ford Bell became president of Washburn Crosby in 1925. A few years later, he joined the company with more than 20 flour mills across the country. The new company was named General Mills. It soon became the largest flour-milling company in the world. General Mills grew, even during the **Great Depression**. The company introduced new products like Bisquick baking mix and Kix cereal.

Cheerioats cereal was introduced around 1941. Four years later, the name was changed to Cheerios. In time, it would become the most popular cereal in the United States.

I guarantee—a perfect cake every time you bake...cake... after cake...after cake!

1940s-1950s Betty Crocker tagline

Betty Crocker radio cooking show

Growth and Change

General Mills continued to grow its line of products in the 1940s. The company made food and supplies for soldiers fighting in World War II. It also began making more packaged foods like cereal and cake mix. After the war ended, televisions became more common. Television commercials helped General Mills reach viewers across the country. Wheaties, Kix, and other General Mills breakfast cereals soon became top sellers.

Mary Lou Retton

WHEATIES

THE BREAKFAST OF CHAMPIONS.

Breakfast of Champions

Wheaties cereal was invented in 1921. It has featured many athletes on its box. In 1984, gymnast Mary Lou Retton was the first female athlete to appear on the box.

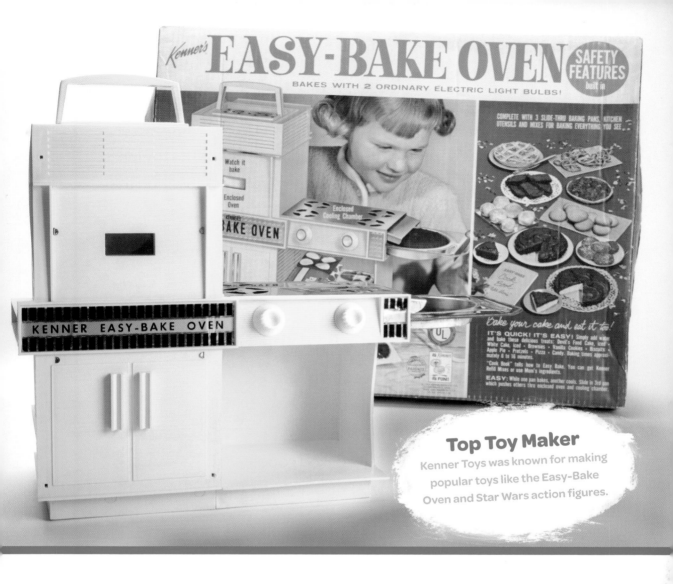

Top Toy Maker

Kenner Toys was known for making popular toys like the Easy-Bake Oven and Star Wars action figures.

General Mills bought more companies in the following decades. It bought Kenner Toys in 1967. Three years later, General Mills entered the restaurant business. It bought the Red Lobster **chain**. It also added new products to the General Mills family. Snack foods and frozen fish were popular additions. Hamburger Helper and Yoplait yogurt later followed. Yearly sales of General Mills products reached more than $2 billion by the mid-1970s!

In the 1980s, company leaders decided that General Mills should focus on food. The company sold its toy lines and expanded its restaurants. General Mills launched the Olive Garden chain in Florida in 1982. Diners loved its Italian food and style. By 1989, around 145 Olive Gardens were open across the country.

In 2001, General Mills made one of its biggest moves yet! It joined with Pillsbury, one of the world's largest food companies. Pillsbury is famous for its baked goods and refrigerated dough. Poppin' Fresh, the Pillsbury Doughboy, is the company's **mascot**. He has starred in more than 600 ads. The addition of Pillsbury made General Mills one of the largest food companies in the world!

Olive Garden

An International Chef

The Pillsbury Doughboy has different names around the world. His German name translates to "The Little Dough Man."

Famous General Mills Brands

Brand Name	Known For
Annie's	natural foods
Betty Crocker	baking mixes
Cheerios	cereal
Chex	cereal
Cocoa Puffs	cereal
Häagen-Dazs	ice cream
Hamburger Helper	boxed dinners
Kix	cereal
Nature Valley	snacks
Old El Paso	Mexican food
Pillsbury	dough
Progresso	soup
Totino's	pizza
Wheaties	cereal
Yoplait	yogurt

Foods People Love Today

Today, General Mills is a worldwide leader in cereal and yogurt sales. Cheerios, Lucky Charms, and Cinnamon Toast Crunch are among the top-selling cold cereals in the United States. Yoplait yogurt comes in 40 flavors. Strawberry, blueberry, and vanilla are favorites. Yoplait Go-Gurt is made especially for kids. Kids can slurp the yogurt from a tube! General Mills continues to create new products, too. Tiny Toast cereal and Progresso **vegan** soups hit shelves in 2016. In early 2017, the company launched the limited-edition Girl Scout Cookie cereal!

Girl Scout Cookie cereal

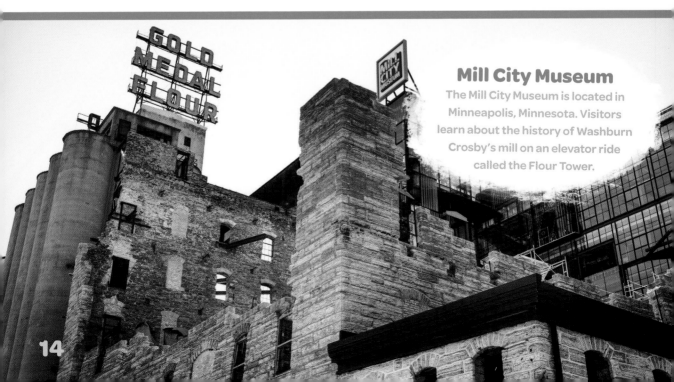

Mill City Museum

The Mill City Museum is located in Minneapolis, Minnesota. Visitors learn about the history of Washburn Crosby's mill on an elevator ride called the Flour Tower.

General Mills is committed to making healthier foods. Many of the company's cereals are made from **whole grains**. Most are free of **artificial** flavors and colors. They are colored and flavored with fruits, vegetables, and spices instead. Cheerios and Kix are low-sugar options. **Organic** foods are also an important part of the General Mills family. The company buys and sells more than 150 million pounds (68 million kilograms) of organic fruits and vegetables each year.

People in more than 100 countries enjoy General Mills products. Betty Crocker, Pillsbury, and other popular brands are found on store shelves around the world. However, some brands are only found in certain areas. Yoki baking mixes and packaged foods are popular in Brazil. In Europe, General Mills cereals are sold under the Nestlé brand. The partnership with Nestlé brings cereals such as Cheerios to people in many countries!

Nestlé cereals

Häagen-Dazs store in Shanghai, China

General Mills products have different flavors around the world, too. In Brazil, General Mills sells flour made from a **tropical** plant called cassava. In Japan, Häagen-Dazs has offered ice cream with flavors such as red bean and purple potatoes. Other unusual flavors are rose and green tea!

Green Tea Häagen-Dazs

Serving Others

General Mills cares about people and the environment. The General Mills **Foundation** was started in 1954. It has given about $2 billion to **charities** around the world. These include Outnumber Hunger. This organization helps feed Americans by collecting food for local **food banks**. Other programs in the United States and Canada provide breakfasts to kids before school. An organization in England collects unused General Mills food for people in need.

General Mills also gives money to organizations that help protect the environment. One focuses on saving bees. Another protects water, soil, and other **natural resources**. General Mills also seeks to help slow **climate change** by reducing **emissions**.

The company helps in other ways, too. It supports worldwide programs that help farmers grow wheat, vanilla, and cocoa. Another program provides tools to communities to make their water safe to drink. General Mills helps people around the world live healthier lives!

Happier Chickens

General Mills promises that by 2025 all of its eggs will come from chickens that do not live in cages.

Cheerios
5 MEALS
Cheerios
Cheerios
DONATED FOOD
NOT FOR RESALE
New York City

General Mills Timeline

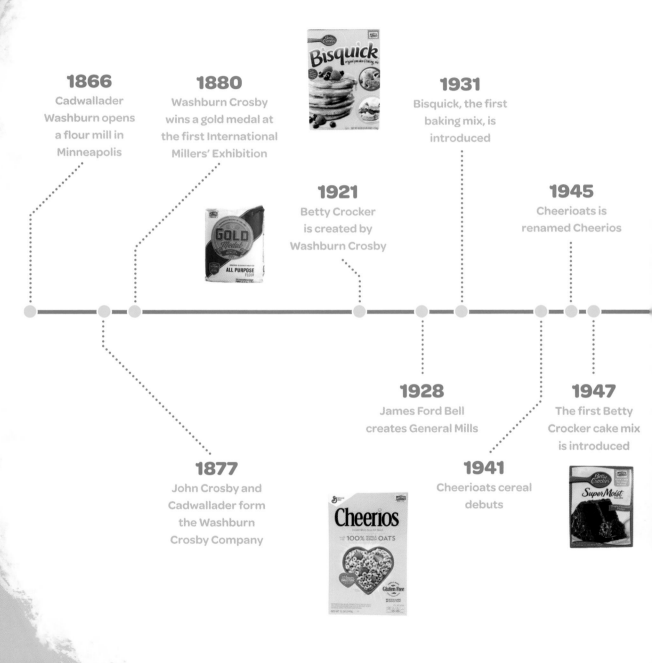

1866
Cadwallader Washburn opens a flour mill in Minneapolis

1880
Washburn Crosby wins a gold medal at the first International Millers' Exhibition

1931
Bisquick, the first baking mix, is introduced

1921
Betty Crocker is created by Washburn Crosby

1945
Cheerioats is renamed Cheerios

1928
James Ford Bell creates General Mills

1947
The first Betty Crocker cake mix is introduced

1877
John Crosby and Cadwallader form the Washburn Crosby Company

1941
Cheerioats cereal debuts

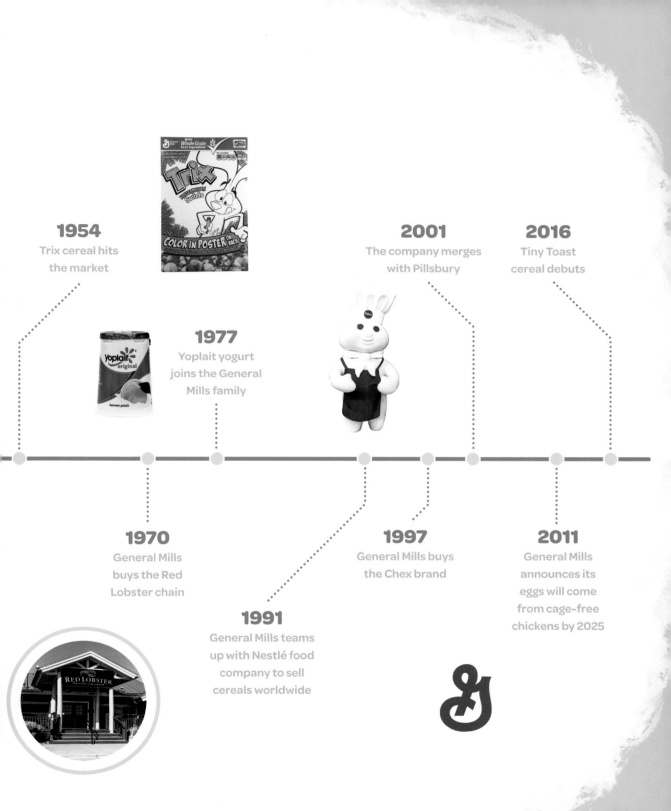

1954
Trix cereal hits
the market

1977
Yoplait yogurt
joins the General
Mills family

2001
The company merges
with Pillsbury

2016
Tiny Toast
cereal debuts

1970
General Mills
buys the Red
Lobster chain

1991
General Mills teams
up with Nestlé food
company to sell
cereals worldwide

1997
General Mills buys
the Chex brand

2011
General Mills
announces its
eggs will come
from cage-free
chickens by 2025

Glossary

advertised—announced or promoted something to get people to buy it

artificial—made by humans rather than by nature

brands—categories of products all made by the same company

chain—a set of related restaurants or businesses with the same name

charities—organizations that help others in need

climate change—a change in global climate patterns due to increasing gases in the earth's atmosphere from human activity

emissions—dangerous fumes

food banks—places that collect and store food for organizations that give it to people free of charge

foundation—an institution that provides funds to charitable organizations

Great Depression—a time in world history when many countries experienced economic crisis

headquarters—a company's main office

logo—a symbol or design that identifies a brand or product

market—the rate or price at which something is sold

mascot—an animal or object used as a symbol by a group or company

natural resources—things that are found in nature that are useful to humans

organic—made without artificial chemicals

tropical—having a hot, wet climate

vegan—made without any animal products

whole grains—grains that have not been processed; whole grains have more nutrients than processed grains.

To Learn More

AT THE LIBRARY

Green, Sara. *Kraft*. Minneapolis, Minn.: Bellwether Media, 2016.

Somervill, Barbara A. *Producing Grains*. Chicago, Ill.: Heinemann Library, 2012.

Spilsbury, Louise. *Grains*. Chicago, Ill.: Heinemann Library, 2009.

ON THE WEB

Learning more about General Mills is as easy as 1, 2, 3.

1. Go to www.factsurfer.com.

2. Enter "General Mills" into the search box.

3. Click the "Surf" button and you will see a list of related web sites.

With factsurfer.com, finding more information is just a click away.

Index

advertising, 5, 8, 10, 12

Bell, James Ford, 8

Betty Crocker, 4, 8, 9, 16

brands, 4, 5, 7, 8, 11, 12, 13, 14, 15, 16, 17

by the numbers, 5

charities, 18, 19

Crosby, John, 7

General Mills Foundation, 18

Gold Medal Flour, 7

Golden Valley, Minnesota, 4, 5

history, 6, 7, 8, 10, 11, 12, 14, 18

international products, 16, 17

Kenner Toys, 11

logo, 4

Mill City Museum, 14

Minneapolis Millers Association, 6

Minneapolis, Minnesota, 6, 7, 14

Pillsbury, 4, 12, 16

products, 4, 5, 7, 8, 10, 11, 12, 13, 14, 15, 16, 17

restaurants, 11, 12

Retton, Mary Lou, 10

sales, 5, 10, 11, 14

taglines, 7, 9

timeline, 20-21

United States, 5, 8, 14, 18

Washburn, Cadwallader, 6, 7

Washburn Crosby Company, 7, 8, 14

worth, 4